INTRODUCING

Machiavelli

Patrick Curry and Oscar Zarate

Edited by Richard Appignanesi

W9-AOZ-883

TOTEM BOOKS

First published in the United States in 1996 by Totem Books
Inquires to PO Box 223, Canal Street Station
New York, NY 10013

Distributed to the trade in the United States
by National Book Network Inc.,
4720 Boston Way, Lanham, Maryland 20706

Text copyright © 1996 Patrick Curry
Illustrations copyright © 1996 Oscar Zarate

Originating editor: Richard Appignanesi

No part of this book may be reproduced in any form, or by any
means, without prior permission in writing from the publisher

ISBN 1 874166 28 5

Library of Congress Catalog Card Number: 95-62414

"Old Nick"

For over four hundred years, Niccolò Machiavelli has been a byword for cynicism, immorality and cruelty in politics. In the 16th century, his first name was often shortened to "Old Nick", the popular nickname for Satan. The Jesuits (themselves accused of Machiavellism by Protestants) called him "the Devil's partner in crime". "Murderous Machiavel" became a favourite reference in Elizabethan plays, including those of Shakespeare.

As Lord Macaulay wrote in 1827, "We doubt whether any name in literary history be so generally odious . . . "

This is how the philosopher Bertrand Russell, in our own century, described Machiavelli's most famous book, **The Prince**.

A HANDBOOK FOR GANGSTERS...

WELL.. AH....

A HANDBOOK FOR STATESMEN!

Fittingly, one of the people Russell probably had in mind, Benito Mussolini, praised it. He had a strong view about whom the new Prince was meant to be and wrote a foreword to a new edition.

This undoubtedly explains the response of Henry Kissinger, for several years the power behind the presidential throne in American politics, to an interviewer's suggestion in 1972 that he was a Machiavellian: "No, not at all!" Was he not influenced by Machiavelli's ideas to at least some extent?

As we shall see, Machiavelli had his fans too, and many of these, like the philosopher Francis Bacon, were not thugs.

WE ARE MUCH BE HOLDEN TO *MACHIAVELLI* AND OTHERS, THAT WRITE WHAT MEN DO, AND NOT WHAT THEY OUGHT TO DO

NICCOLO MACHIAVELLI WROTE ABOUT THE WORLD WE LIVE IN, MAN, THE WAY IT REALLY IS, WITHOUT ALL THE BULLSHIT.

MIKE TYSON

But Machiavelli's bad press continues today. **The Prince**, says the **Guardian** newspaper, is "the ultimate handbook in political expediency". And the latest edition of **Chambers English Dictionary** has Machiavellian as an adjective, meaning "politically cunning and unscrupulous, seeking power or advantage at any price; amoral and opportunist".

So what was Machiavelli: evil genius or brilliant political theorist? And what does he have to tell us today? To answer that you have to know *who* he was, and what he wrote in relation to his own time and problems. **5**

Renaissance Florence

The golden age of Florence was in the 15th century. Florence's wealth became legendary. Its coin, the florin, was respected everywhere, and its merchants conducted business far and wide, first in the wool industry and then in silk and trade with the East. One of the richest and most successful families was the Medici. Originally from the Mugello valley, they amassed great wealth as merchant bankers and became bankers to the Papacy. Soon their ambitions extended to politics, the Papacy itself, and the rulership of their native city. But the Medici were also renowned as generous patrons of the arts and humanities. They were no petty tyrants.

A *florin*

SIENA →

ROME →

Emblem of Florence

This combination of commerce, culture and enlightened despotism made Florence the Renaissance equivalent of Athens in classical antiquity, another turning point in European culture and civilization. **7**

Thanks to the patronage of wealthy merchant families like the Medici, in a time of almost unprecedented creativity and optimism, Florence became the principal centre for Western arts and sciences. Around 1420, Filippo Brunelleschi designed the huge dome of the cathedral of Santa Maria del Fiore, near the Tower by Giotto, and, together with Ghiberti, oversaw its construction. It was completed in 1436, although the lantern was not finished until after Brunelleschi's death. Along with Alberti, he also developed linear perspective.

Discoveries in anatomy, combined with artistic creativity, distinguished the sculptures of Donatello and the paintings of Piero della Francesca. Botticelli's **Birth of Venus** and **Primavera** exquisitely expressed the new interest in pagan classical subjects.

Leonardo da Vinci was a Florentine and in his life and work perhaps best exemplifies its intellectual curiosity, humane scepticism, and sensitivity. He rubbed shoulders in Florence with Michelangelo, the giant of Western sculpture and painting, as he developed his mastery of the human form.

And, incredibly, the still younger Raphael – from Urbino, but painting in Florence – visited and watched both men's work in progress.

Raphael

Michelangelo

At the same time, ideas about the frontiers of the known physical world were also being challenged. Christopher Columbus set sail on his first historic trip in 1492. Shortly afterwards, he was followed by a Florentine, Amerigo Vespucci, who gave his name to the Americas.

In philosophy, Cosimo de'Medici commissioned Marsilio Ficino to translate the mystical writings of Hermes Trismegistus and Plato's dialogues into Latin. Ficino upturned the old Aristotelian–Christian synthesis with his translations. Lorenzo the Magnificent continued this support, underwriting the foundation of the Platonic Academy, Ficino's own work, and the short but extraordinary career of Pico della Mirandola, whom Machiavelli described as "a man almost divine". Pico's meditations on the dignity of man, combining Christian theology, Platonic philosophy and hermetic magic, set the seal on Renaissance humanism.

Marsilio Ficino

PLATO DIALOGVE

Pico della Mirandola

What is Humanism?

The word comes from the Latin *humanitas*, from *homo*, man. As a movement, it can be said to have started with the 14th-century poet Petrarch, the son of a Florentine exile. The humanists' heroes were the poets, scholars and orators of classical republican Rome: Cicero, Horace and Virgil. Renaissance humanism was not anti-Christian: it perceived a universal harmony underlying both classical pagan philosophy (especially that of Plato, Plotinus and their followers) and Christianity.

At the centre of the humanist world was not God, however, but the human being (in some versions a divine humanity); not the next world but this; not the ineffable individual soul but public and social life. There was faith, but mainly in the idea that with wisdom, skill and effort the world could be changed: "virtu vince fortuna" (ability wins over fortune).

Civic Republicanism: the Good Citizen

Humanism was closely identified with classical (that is, pagan) and civic (social and political) **republicanism**.

THE GOOD MAN IS IDENTIFIED WITH THE CITIZEN, WITH THE RESULT THAT HIS GOODNESS, RATHER THAN BEING PURELY INDIVIDUAL, DEPENDS CRUCIALLY ON THAT OF OTHERS.

An attempt was made to integrate the classical virtues – typically justice, temperance, wisdom and fortitude – with the later Christian ones of humility and righteousness. Nonetheless, this position involved a sharp rejection of Augustinian or medieval Christianity, with its emphasis on original sin, the omnipotence of God, and individual salvation.

Birth of Machiavelli

Niccolò Machiavelli was born in Florence on 3 May 1469 to an old and moderately wealthy family. He was the third son of his father, Bernardo, an educated humanist, who practised law.

He received the best humanist schooling of his day, culminating in attendance at lectures at the University of Florence. Humanist education continued with the system that had become institutionalized in the Middle Ages consisting of the seven liberal arts: the **trivium** (logic, rhetoric and grammar) plus the **quadrivium** (arithmetic, geometry, astronomy and music). Special attention, however, was paid to classical Latin literature, and the study of ancient history, philosophy and rhetoric.

Humanism was not only an intellectual movement. Educated humanists held many of the most important positions in Florentine government.

A Divided Italy

Florence was one of several city-states on the Italian mainland which dominated the surrounding areas. They included Milan, Venice, Florence, papal Rome, Genoa, Siena and Naples. From the early 15th century, Florence ruled most of Tuscany, except Lucca and Siena. Pisa, as Florence's only outlet to the sea, had a particular strategic importance and was the object of continual struggle between the Florentines and the Pisans who were attempting to become independent.

OPTIMISM IS COMMERCE AND CULTURE — THAT'S THE GOOD NEWS. NOW FOR THE BAD NEWS!

Despite its cultural and artistic achievements, Renaissance Italy was about to enter a period of intense political chaos and upheaval. It was this that came to dominate Machiavelli's life and work.

Nation States and the Holy Roman Empire

Meanwhile, a threat to divided Italy was developing in the growth of "modern" nation-states in nearby France and Spain.

Another major player was the Holy Roman Empire occupying most of what we now know as Germany and Austria. It began in 800 when Charlemagne was crowned Emperor of the West by Pope Leo III and persisted until 1806 when Napoleon conquered the last imperial territories.

Guelfs and Ghibellines

Florence had a long and troubled political history. Throughout the 1200s it was embroiled in the war between the Guelf party on the side of the Pope (which included Florence) and the Ghibellines on the side of the Holy Roman Emperor (including Siena, Lucca and Pisa). At the end of the 13th century, the Florentine Guelfs themselves divided into two factions: the Whites (against the Pope) and the Blacks (his supporters). Machiavelli comments on this internecine factional split in his **History of Florence** (1525).

NOT EVEN A VICTORIOUS FACTION EVER REMAINED UNITED, EXCEPT SO LONG AS THE OPPOSING FACTION WAS VIGOROUS. BUT WHEN A BEATEN FACTION WAS DESTROYED, SINCE THE PARTY IN POWER NO LONGER FELT ANY FEAR THAT COULD RESTRICT IT AND HAD NO LAW OF ITS OWN TO CHECK IT, THE VICTOR BECAME DIVIDED.

A civil war broke out between the White and Black factions of the Guelf party. The Whites lost and in 1302 many found themselves cast into exile, with their homes and property destroyed, and under threat of death if they were ever caught within Florentine jurisdiction. Among these was Italy's greatest poet, Dante Alighieri, who never returned to Florence.

Dante aptly described the bitterness of exile in his **Divine Comedy**.

Thou shalt by sharp experience be aware
How salt the bread of strangers is, how hard
The up and down of someone else's stair...

Well shall it be for thee to have preferred
Making a party of thyself alone.

PARADISE XVII 58 - 69

DOES HE PREDICT MY OWN EXILE FROM FLORENCE?

The Dream of Republican Liberty

The struggle between Guelphs and Ghibellines, in as well as around Florence, continued throughout the 14th century. And there were other crises. In 1342, for example, the tyrannical Walter de Brienne, "Duke of Athens", seized power, only to be expelled after a popular revolt the next year.

PITY THE FLORENTINES, WHO CANNOT KEEP THEIR LIBERTY AND YET CANNOT ENDURE SERVITUDE.

The structure of Florence's late medieval government was a complex arrangement of one large council, with about a thousand members, and other smaller councils, of which the most powerful was the Signory. These were variously elected by tax-paying citizens, members of guilds, and the common people. The chief minister was the Gonfalonier of Justice (so named because he bore the Gonfalone, the city's standard).

...COUNTRIES GENERALLY GO FROM ORDER TO DISORDER AND THEN FROM DISORDER MOVE BACK TO ORDER... BECAUSE ABILITY BRINGS FORTH QUIET; QUIET, LAZINESS; LAZINESS, DISORDER, DISORDER, RUIN; AND LIKEWISE FROM RUIN COMES ORDER; FROM ORDER, ABILITY; FROM THE LAST GLORY AND GOOD FORTUNE.

FROM *The History of Florence*

The Medici take Power

The Medici family came to power in 1434 as a result of a struggle between the most powerful families in Florence. Slowly, they began to make inroads in this loosely democratic system. Cosimo de' Medici pre-selected candidates for the Signory and after 1458 replaced the old councils with special and personal ones. In 1480, Lorenzo devised a new council of 70 who were selected from the old regime and whose powers were extended every five years; this in turn elected a smaller number of ministers to advise the prince in running the state, so the importance of the Signory declined yet again.

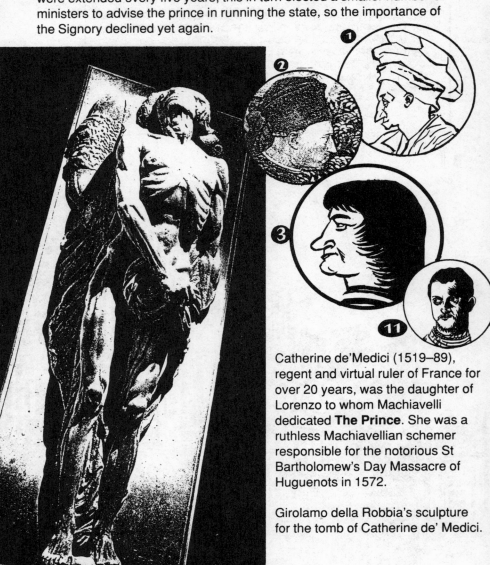

Catherine de'Medici (1519–89), regent and virtual ruler of France for over 20 years, was the daughter of Lorenzo to whom Machiavelli dedicated **The Prince**. She was a ruthless Machiavellian schemer responsible for the notorious St Bartholomew's Day Massacre of Huguenots in 1572.

Girolamo della Robbia's sculpture for the tomb of Catherine de' Medici.

~ The MEDICI ~

GIOVANNI *di* BICCI 1360~1429

① COSIMO 1389~1464 ^1434~64

LORENZO 1394~1440

② PIERO 1418~69 ^1464~69

⑪ COSIMO II 1519~74 ^1537~74

③ LORENZO *the Magnificent* 1449~92 ^1469~92

GIULIANO 1453~78

⑧ GIULIO *became* CLEMENT VII 1478~1534 ^1519-23

④ PIERO II 1471~1503 ^1492-94

⑤ GIOVANNI 1475~1521 *became* LEO·X ^1512-13

GIULIANO II 1478~1516 **⑥** ^1513

R

⑦ LORENZO III *Duke of Urbino* 1492~1519 ^1513-19

⑨ IPPOLITO 1511~35 ^1523-27

R

CATHERINE 1519~89 *Married* HENRY II *of France*

ALESSANDRO 1511~37 **⑩** ^1531-37

① = EFFECTIVE HEAD OF STATE OF FLORENCE (& DATES THEREOF)

R ~ REPUBLICS: 1494 TO 1512 1527 TO 1530

The Republic Reborn

Lorenzo de' Medici, "the Magnificent", who assumed power in the year of Machiavelli's birth, gave Florence her last relatively stable and prosperous period for many years to come.

MY DEATH IN *1492* WOULD SOON LEAD TO... A NEW REPUBLIC!

The army of Charles VIII of France entered Italy to assert his claim to the throne of Naples. Lorenzo's successor, Piero II, unwisely sided with Naples against the French king. The French invaded Florence in 1494. Piero was banished in disgrace by the angry citizens who immediately established a republic and restored the former Great Council of 1000.

Savonarola

The republic lasted from 1494 to 1512. Its effective ruler in the first four years was the fiery Dominican preacher Girolamo Savonarola (1452–98) who held no formal political position. Savonarola had been invited to Florence in 1490 by Lorenzo on the strength of his reputation. A charismatic preacher, he issued denunciations of worldly corruption in both society and church.

Savonarola managed to exploit both the discontent of the city's increasingly disenfranchised masses and their fears about the future. **27**

The Bonfire of Vanities

Savonarola's goal was to combine religious revivalism and what we would now call fundamentalism – attacking both the commerce and the culture of humanism – with a stern theocratic republicanism that aimed at realizing God's plan on earth. Such was his popular following that the annual Carnival of 1497 was capped, at his urging, by a "pyre of vanities": an enormous bonfire of "worldly" attachments – books, pictures, jewellery. His influence upon the élite was enormous too: Botticelli burned his nude studies of Simonetta . . .

The people began to tire of Savonarola's strict regime, and a declining economy caused second thoughts. His reforming zeal made an enemy of the Pope, who finally excommunicated him and placed the entire city of Florence under an interdict. Savonarola's political allies, sensing a change in the wind, gradually deserted him, and in 1498 the Pope brought off charges of heresy against him. Savonarola ended his life in a bonfire in the same square as his "pyre of vanities".

THE UNARMED PROPHET ALWAYS COMES TO GRIEF.

NOBODY SHOULD START A REVOLUTION IN A CITY IN THE BELIEF THAT LATER HE CAN STOP IT AT WILL OR REGULATE IT AS HE LIKES.

By now Machiavelli was 29, an ambitious and intelligent young man.

"Of middle height, slender figure, sparkling eyes, dark hair, rather a small head, a slightly aquiline nose, a tightly closed mouth; all about him bore the impress of a very acute observer and thinker . . . He could not easily rid himself of the sarcastic expression continually playing round his mouth and flashing from his eyes . . ."

Machiavelli Goes to Work

In June 1498, Machiavelli's chance came. Probably through influential humanist friends of his father, now in government, he was elected by the Great Council to an important post in the civil service, that of second chancellor.

Then, a month later, he was appointed secretary to the Ten of War – the committee in charge of Florence's foreign policy and military

MY JOB WAS TO REPORT TO THE *TEN* ON SENSITIVE DIPLOMATIC MATTERS, AND ACT AS THEIR MESSENGER IN ANY NEGOTIATIONS.

Machiavelli's job involved taking real responsibility in complex and tricky negotiations, the course of which could materially affect Florence: as much a minister as a civil servant, in our terms. Machiavelli took it very seriously, working hard and conscientiously.

The Diplomat at Work

In 1500, Florence launched a campaign to recover Pisa, which had used the chaos caused by the French invasion to declare its independence.

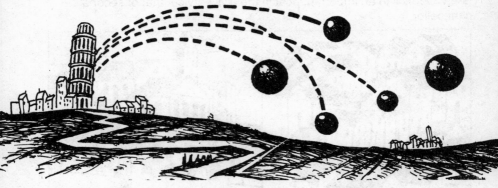

But the mainly mercenary troops failed dismally, and Machiavelli spent six months in the court of Louis XII, trying to convince the French to help recover Pisa. The patriotic Machiavelli was shocked to discover that the French regarded Florence with contempt and amusement.

The next year, Machiavelli found time to marry Marietta Corsini. They seem to have had an affectionate relationship, and six children eventually followed. But he wasn't home for long.

Pope Alexander VI had made his son, Cesare Borgia, or Duke Valentino, the Duke of Romagna; and Borgia began a lightning military campaign to carve out his own domain. This just happened to border on Florentine territory, which worried the government considerably, and, in October of 1502, they sent Machiavelli to negotiate terms with the Duke.

33

Who Were the Borgias?

Cesare Borgia (1476–1507) and Lucrezia Borgia (1480–1519) were both the illegitimate children of Rodrigo Borgia (1431–1503), who became Pope Alexander VI in 1492 .

Lucrezia was as notorious as her brother for her involvement in the power- politics and intrigue of her day.

I PROCEEDED UNHINDERED FROM MY LATEST SUDDEN WIDOWHOOD TO THE NEXT AMBITIOUS MARRIAGE.

Cesare's father made him a cardinal at 17, but soon released him from his vows.

MY SON DOESN'T SEEM CUT OUT FOR THE SPIRITUAL LIFE.

With Dad's help, Cesare became captain general of the Papal armies in Romagna.

Cesare Borgia's Genius

Machiavelli was very impressed by Cesare Borgia and warned the Ten that here was "a new power in Italy". Typical of Cesare's effectiveness (and ruthlessness) was the way he dealt with a lieutenant, Rimirro de Orco, whose pointless savagery was jeopardizing his rule in Romagna. The offender was murdered and left in the main public square.

Shortly afterwards, Cesare learned of a plot to assassinate him in Senigallia.

> HE WENT THERE, INVITED THE PLOTTERS TO DINNER, AND HAD THEM SLAUGHTERED AS THEY ATE.

Machiavelli described all this in his letters in tones of wonder and even admiration.

Leonardo and Machiavelli

In 1502, as Machiavelli's diplomatic mission arrived, Cesare hired Leonardo da Vinci as his chief military architect and engineer. Both men accompanied Cesare during his successful campaigns of 1502 and were at Senigallia during his slaughter of the schemers.

The two men – Machiavelli, the student of ruthless power, and Leonardo, the peaceful vegetarian – were united by the Renaissance spirit of curiosity and objective inquiry. Man was the object of Machiavelli's inquiry; nature Leonardo's. They got on brilliantly well together and became good friends.

LATER, I USED MY INFLUENCE TO OBTAIN A MAJOR COMMISSION IN FLORENCE FOR LEONARDO — A FRESCO DEPICTING THE BATTLE OF ANGHIARI — ON ONE OF THE WALLS OF THE GRAND COUNCIL CHAMBER IN THE PALAZZO VECCHIO.

A Change of Fortune

But in 1502, the Duke's fortunes changed radically, and all his gains counted for nothing. For, in August, the Duke's father Alexander VI died, followed after one month by his short-lived successor Pius III. Machiavelli was immediately sent to Rome to report on the next papal election. It was won by Julius II, whom Cesare Borgia had supported in return for a promise to appoint him head of the papal armies.

AH, BUT I REMEMBER WHAT I SUFFERED UNDER BORGIA'S FATHER...SO, TO HELL WITH MY PROMISE!

NOW FOR THE FINISHING TOUCHES...

Raphael

Typically, instead of condemning this as immoral, Machiavelli commended it as astute.

I CRITICIZE BORGIA INSTEAD FOR POOR JUDGEMENT AND RELYING TOO MUCH ON HIS USUAL GOOD FORTUNE.

At the same time, the Duke fell ill; and, without Papal support, his empire started to fall apart. By November, Machiavelli could assure the Ten that they need worry about him no longer.

Secretary of the Militia

In 1502, Piero Soderini, a respected humanist and friend of Machiavelli, had been elected Gonfalonier for life. At first he was very effective, uniting internal factions and eventually recovering Pisa, lost in 1494.

Machiavelli's scheme was accepted, and in 1507 a new committee, the "Nine Militia" was formed with Machiavelli as secretary. Pisa was regained in 1509.

Meanwhile, Machiavelli was sent on new missions to the court of Pope Julius II, the great patron of Michelangelo, whom he commissioned to paint the Sistine Chapel.

MICHELANGELO, HAVE A LOOK AT THOSE WALLS - DO SOMETHING ABOUT IT, WILL YOU?

JULIUS IS DYNAMIC. HE HAS RECOVERED THE FORMER PAPAL PROTECTORATES OF PERUGIA AND BOLOGNA. I FEAR WHAT HIS AMBITIONS HAVE IN STORE FOR FLORENCE...

Machiavelli also visited the court of the Holy Roman Emperor, Maximilian, who struck him as weak and ineffective.

The Return of the Medici

In the face of rapidly shifting circumstances, Soderini clung too long to his customary pro-French and anti-military policy. In 1511, Pope Julius concluded an alliance with King Ferdinand of Spain against France, and the next summer Spanish troops attacked and pushed back the French beyond Milan.

SODERINI AND THE FLORENTINE LEADERS FAILED TO SEE WHICH WAY THE WIND WAS BLOWING..

Florence was encircled, its small and inexperienced militia stood no chance against the tough Spanish infantry. In September 1512, the city surrendered and Soderini fled.

The young republic was dissolved and the Mèdici, under Giuliano II, reinstalled by the Spanish in 1513. The Medici remained in power until 1737. Republican dreams of liberty were completely shattered.

Machiavelli's Downfall

That November, the blow fell. Machiavelli was dismissed from the Chancery. Three months later, in February 1513, he was accused falsely of conspiracy. Arrested and imprisoned for 22 days, Machiavelli was tortured for information by being subjected to six drops from the *strappado*, a device in which its victims were raised by their arms tied behind their back and then suddenly released. The result was extremely painful and usually resulted in broken shoulders.

He was released in March. Julius II had died, and his successor, Cardinal Giovanni de' Medici, became Leo X. The extraordinary success of the Medici family was thus renewed. Florence became a papal protectorate and a general amnesty was declared.

Shaken and unemployed, Machiavelli retired to his small family farm at Sant'Andrea, 7 miles south of Florence.

Machiavelli at Sant'Andrea

These were difficult days for Machiavelli, accustomed as he was to life in the city, within reach of the levers of political power that so fascinated him. In a letter to his friend Francesco Vettori in Rome, written on 10 December 1513, Machiavelli describes his new way of life.

I PASS THE DAY OVERSEEING THE WORK ON MY FARM...
READING POETRY OUTSIDE ("EITHER DANTE OR PETRARCH")
...GOSSIPING WITH THE VILLAGERS...

AFTER DINNER WITH MY FAMILY, I GO TO THE LOCAL INN TO CHAT AND PLAY GAMES WITH WORKING MEN.

WHEN IT GETS DARK, HOWEVER ...

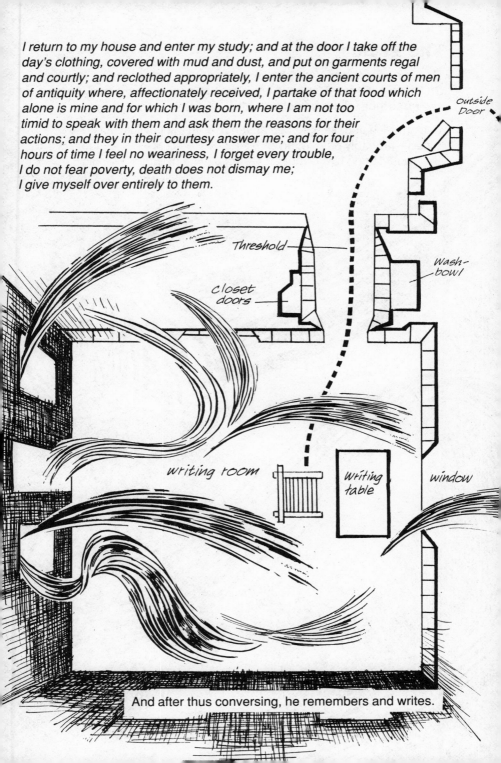

I return to my house and enter my study; and at the door I take off the day's clothing, covered with mud and dust, and put on garments regal and courtly; and reclothed appropriately, I enter the ancient courts of men of antiquity where, affectionately received, I partake of that food which alone is mine and for which I was born, where I am not too timid to speak with them and ask them the reasons for their actions; and they in their courtesy answer me; and for four hours of time I feel no weariness, I forget every trouble, I do not fear poverty, death does not dismay me; I give myself over entirely to them.

Outside Door

Threshold

Wash-bowl

closet doors

writing room

Writing table

window

And after thus conversing, he remembers and writes.

The Prince

Thus, as he wrote to Vettori in December, "I have composed a little book, **On Principalities**." This "little book" was to become immensely famous as **The Prince**, although not until after his death.

Machiavelli hated his enforced absence from the political action and hoped – probably naïvely, given his republican credentials – that his tract would bring him favour and re-employment with the Medicis.

CICERO

Tito Livio

In its general form, **The Prince** belongs to a well-established Renaissance genre of advice-books for princes. Machiavelli writes very much in the tradition of classical and civic humanism. But in certain respects – ones that shocked his contemporaries – he broke decisively with that tradition.

Machiavelli extols the ancient examples of leaders like Moses, Cyrus (founder of the Persian empire), Theseus (the legendary King of Athens), and Romulus (the mythical founder of Rome), as well as the more historical Philip of Macedonia, who paved the way for Alexander the Great.

BUT IN THESE CORRUPT TIMES, THE MEDICIS, UNEXPECTEDLY RESTORED TO POWER BY SPANISH ARMS, ARE MUCH MORE TYPICAL.

H'M, NOT VERY FLATTERING TO THE MEDICIS!

AH, IT'S YOU — MY FUTURE ME. SIT DOWN, LET'S TALK.

New dominions offer particular problems to rulers, for no matter how powerful one's armies, the prince also needs the goodwill of the people. Otherwise he has no helpers in times of adversity.

BUT THERE IS A BOTTOM LINE WHEN ESTABLISHING A NEW RULE...

MEN MUST BE EITHER PAMPERED OR CRUSHED, BECAUSE THEY CAN GET REVENGE FOR SMALL INJURIES, BUT NOT FOR GRIEVOUS ONES. SO ANY INJURY A PRINCE DOES A MAN SHOULD BE OF SUCH A KIND THAT THERE IS NO FEAR OF REVENGE.

The leaders of the Roman Republic provide a good example of the foresight needed for stability, because, by the time trouble is obvious to everyone, it is usually too late to end it. So they never allowed troubles to develop very far.

THE REASON, WHICH I TACTFULLY DID NOT SPELL OUT HERE, IS THAT A REPUBLIC MOST FULLY AND TRULY ACCORDS WITH HUMAN NATURE.

THERE IS NOTHING MORE DIFFICULT TO HANDLE, MORE DOUBTFUL OF SUCCESS AND MORE DANGEROUS TO CARRY THROUGH THAN INITIATING CHANGES IN A STATE'S CONSTITUTION.

Given these difficulties, Machiavelli tells the would-be prince, it is not enough merely to be persuasive. One must be able to stand alone without depending on others, and if necessary to force the issue.

YES, JUST LOOK AT WHAT GORBACHEV STARTED IN RUSSIA AND WHAT YELTSIN HAS TO FINISH!

Among his other contemporaries, Machiavelli singles out Cesare Borgia as worthy of particular attention. He praises the way the Duke acted swiftly, decisively and if necessary ruthlessly, playing off France, the Italian city-states and the Papacy against each other, suppressing conspiracies, and laying strong foundations for the future.

UNTIL THE SUDDEN DEATH OF HIS FATHER THE POPE, AND HIS OWN ILLNESS, CESARE'S CAMPAIGN TO CARVE OUT A NEW PRINCIPALITY SEEMED LIKELY TO SUCCEED.

IF WHAT HE INSTITUTED WAS OF NO AVAIL, THIS WAS NOT HIS FAULT BUT AROSE FROM THE EXTRAORDINARY AND INORDINATE MALICE OF FORTUNE.

IT IS IMPORTANT TO NOTE THAT I DID NOT ADVOCATE POWER, OR THE POWER TACTICS OF BORGIA, AS AN END IN ITSELF. THE ONLY POINT OF POWER, IN MY VIEW, IS IN ORDER TO CREATE AND MAINTAIN A STRONG STATE, CAPABLE OF PROTECTING THE FREEDOM AND SECURITY OF ITS CITIZENS.

Likewise, he did not sanction violence for its own sake:

EXACTLY. IT CANNOT BE CALLED PROWESS TO KILL FELLOW CITIZENS, TO BETRAY FRIENDS, TO BE TREACHEROUS, PITILESS, IRRELIGIOUS. THESE WAYS CAN WIN A PRINCE POWER BUT NOT GLORY.

On the contrary, Machiavelli differentiated between purposeful cruelty and mindless, indiscriminate or perpetual cruelty. Similarly, any violence involved in taking over a corrupt state and restoring it to order must be inflicted once and for all, not continually.

The Whims of Fortune

One of the most important concepts in Machiavelli's work is that of **Fortune**, a word which includes the ideas of a force that intervenes uncontrollably in our lives, luck (either good or bad), and simply unforeseen changes in circumstances. He admits that the power of Fortune is very great; this had been especially evident in the turmoil of Italy in his day, with its sweeping and unpredictable changes.

· I COMPARE FORTUNE TO A RIVER PRONE TO FLOODS.

When it is flowing quietly in its normal course, that is the time to take precautions, building dykes and embankments. Then the flood, if and when it comes, will be less violent; whereas, unresisted, it will sweep everything before it.

FORTUNE EXPLAINS WHY TWO PEOPLE BEHAVING IN OPPOSITE WAYS — ONE CAUTIOUS, THE OTHER HEADSTRONG — CAN BOTH SUCCEED.

There are examples of leaders proceeding in identical ways, yet one succeeds while the other fails. The one who can adapt his policy to the times prospers, whereas the one who cannot and thus provokes a clash ooes not.

I REMEMBER ALSO CONCEIVING OF FORTUNE AS A GODDESS...

YES, IN ANCIENT ROME SHE WAS THE DAUGHTER OF JUPITER AND THE OBJECT OF POPULAR CULT-WORSHIP.

Machiavelli overturns the Christian interpretation of previous centuries, which turned Fortune into either blind chance or divine (but unknowable) Providence. He returns to the pagan classical view that Fortune can be influenced, and even mastered, albeit not forever.

ALTHOUGH FICKLE, FORTUNE OFFERS GREAT GIFTS AS WELL AS RUIN: NAMELY *HONOUR, GLORY* AND *FAME.*

The Fortunes of War

Machiavelli devotes a long section of **The Prince** to military organization. The reason (stated with typical authority and self-confidence) is that "The main foundations of every state, new states as well as ancient or composite ones, are good laws and good arms; and because you cannot have good laws without good arms, and where there are good arms, good laws will inevitably follow, I shall not discuss laws but give my attention to arms."

Machiavelli was particularly scathing about the practice, then common throughout Italy, of relying upon mercenary troops.

THEIR ALLEGIANCE IS FICKLE, THEIR OWN SELF-PRESERVATION PRECEDES THE CAUSE OF THEIR EMPLOYERS, AND IT IS MORE IN THEIR INTEREST TO EXTEND THAN TO END ANY WAR.

WHEN CHARLES VIII OF FRANCE INVADED ITALY, FOR EXAMPLE, MERCENARY SOLDIERS OFFERED NO EFFECTIVE RESISTANCE.

ROME AND SPARTA ENDURED FOR CENTURIES ON THE STRENGTH OF THEIR OWN ARMS.

THE CONTEMPORARY SWISS ARE STRONGLY ARMED AND COMPLETELY FREE. THE CONNECTION IS NOT ACCIDENTAL.

With the exaggeration he sometimes used in order to make a point, Machiavelli therefore states that a prince must make his first and even only concern . . .

Machiavelli justifies his realism and lack of sentimentality by arguing that his interest is things as they are, not as they are idealistically imagined or wished to be.

MANY WRITERS HAVE DREAMED UP IDEAL COUNTRIES, BUT THE GULF BETWEEN THEM AND REALITY IS SO GREAT THAT TO NEGLECT WHAT IS ACTUALLY DONE FOR WHAT SHOULD BE DONE IS SIMPLY TO INVITE SELF-DESTRUCTION.

THE FACT IS THAT A MAN WHO WANTS TO ACT VIRTUOUSLY IN EVERY WAY NECESSARILY COMES TO GRIEF AMONG SO MANY WHO ARE NOT VIRTUOUS.

TAXES

Indeed, the prince will find that some supposed virtues will ruin him and lose the state, whereas some apparent vices will bring security and prosperit

Similarly, a prince must not mind if he is thought cruel, as long as he is able to keep his subjects loyal and united.

MAKING AN EXAMPLE OF ONE OR TWO OFFENDERS IS KINDER THAN BEING TOO COMPASSIONATE, AND ALLOWING DISORDERS TO DEVELOP INTO MURDER AND CHAOS WHICH AFFECTS THE WHOLE COMMUNITY.

BUT I AM NOT RECOMMENDING CRUELTY OR VIOLENCE AS SUCH.

Indeed, he specifically criticizes the Greek tyrant Agathocles, whose "countless crimes forbid his being honoured among men." The point is that the prince must be able to use extreme methods, as and when necessary, to restore the viability of a community.

Machiavelli asks whether it is better for a ruler to be feared or loved.

IDEALLY, A RULER WOULD LIKE TO BE BOTH FEARED AND LOVED.

THE ANSWER IS THAT ONE WOULD LIKE TO BE BOTH; BUT BECAUSE IT IS DIFFICULT TO COMBINE THEM, IT IS FAR BETTER TO BE FEARED THAN LOVED.

The reason, revealing his pessimistic view of human nature, is this: men "are ungrateful, fickle, liars, and deceivers, cowardly and greedy; while you treat them well, they are yours . . . but when you are in danger they turn against you." Consequently, they worry less about doing harm to someone who is merely loved than to someone they fear, and from whom they can expect swift and sure punishment.

Machiavelli's prince is an innovator without the support of ancient custom and the protection it offers against unbridled Fortune. He must therefore act quickly; it simply takes too long to become loved in a way that can be relied upon.

Nonetheless, Machiavelli distinguishes sharply between fear and hatred. One should indeed be feared, but try not to be not hated; that is very dangerous and should be avoided.

The Lion and the Fox

Machiavelli says that there are two ways of fighting: by law, which is the way of men, and by force, which is that of beasts.

BUT I DELIGHTED IN BREAKING WITH THE HUMANIST TRADITION OF WRITERS LIKE CICERO BY ARGUING THAT THE LAW IS SOMETIMES INADEQUATE.

A PRINCE MUST UNDERSTAND HOW TO MAKE A NICE USE OF THE BEAST AND THE MAN.

The beasts Machiavelli recommends as models are just those rejected as unworthy by the humanists: the fox, for his cunning and craftiness, and the lion, for his brute strength.

Pagan Virtù and Christian Virtue

Machiavelli's general advice is to be bold rather than timid. In the words of the maxim, "Fortune favours the brave."

...BEING A WOMAN, SHE FAVOURS YOUNG MEN, BECAUSE THEY ARE LESS CIRCUM-SPECT AND MORE ARDENT, AND BECAUSE THEY COMMAND HER WITH GREATER AUDACITY.

THE WORD DOES NOT DESCRIBE A "GOOD" OR "VIRTUOUS" PERSON IN THE USUAL SENSE.

This ability – call it vigour, prowess, bravery, pride, courage, strength – was what Machiavelli called **virtù** (from the Latin *virtus*, itself from *vir*, man). In other words, **virtù** describes the qualities desirable for a man which include a certain ruthlessness.

70

In his opinion, not only individuals but nations could possess **virtù**. Having it did not guarantee success; but without it failure was certain, since the only alternative involves depending purely on Fortune. "Therefore the only sound, sure and enduring methods of defence are those based on your own **virtù**."

Here, Machiavelli shattered the classical belief, articulated by Cicero.

VIRTÙ CONSISTS ESPECIALLY OF ALWAYS ACTING HONOURABLY AND MORALLY — "HONESTY IS THE BEST POLICY".

SENECA

IT IS INCONCEIVABLE THAT ANY RULER COULD ACTUALLY BE LIKE THAT, IN A WORLD DOMINATED BY MEN WHO ARE NOT GOOD, AND SURVIVE FOR LONG.

AN EFFECTIVE RULER WILL NOT BE MERCIFUL.

CESARE BORGIA WAS ACCOUNTED CRUEL, BUT HIS APPARENT CRUELTY BROUGHT THE ROMAGNA PEACE AND STABILITY.

Machiavelli's idea of **virtù** is the key to achieving success amid the changes of Fortune. He redefined it, however, to include being willing to do wrong and use either force (the lion) or cunning (the fox) when the circumstances make it necessary, as well as the art of hypocrisy: that is, knowing how to appear moral all the while.

Machiavelli's **virtù**, as the will and ability to do whatever it takes to secure the state, thus came to mean precisely the opposite of **virtue** in the usual (Christian) sense!

The Fine Balance of Power

Being well ordered and well armed is enough to repel external aggression. But, to be free from the danger of internal plots and subversion, a prince must keep his nobles respectful and the people content.

Princes must try to prevent hatred becoming universal. For example, they should try to retain the loyalty of the most powerful classes (such as the nobility and military).

THE PRINCE SHOULD RESTRAIN HIMSELF FROM INFLICTING GRAVE INJURY ON ANYONE IN HIS SERVICE WHOM HE HAS CLOSE TO HIM IN HIS AFFAIRS OF STATE.

General hatred and scorn have been the ruin of even the most powerful Roman emperors; admiration and prestige the making of others.

SO, THE BEST FORTRESS THAT EXISTS IS TO AVOID BEING HATED BY THE PEOPLE.

One of Machiavelli's model new princes was Ferdinand of Aragon, the King of Spain.

HIS MILITARY CAMPAIGNS IN EUROPE AND INDIA HAVE KEPT HIS SUBJECTS AMAZED AND IMPRESSED, AND WON HIM A GREAT REPUTATION.

PRINCES WHO ARE IRRESOLUTE LIKE PRESIDENT CLINTON, USUALLY FOLLOW THE PATH OF NEUTRALITY IN ORDER TO ESCAPE IMMEDIATE DANGER, AND USUALLY THEY COME TO GRIEF.

WELL, GEE... UH, HMM...

Besides, all courses of action are risky, so prudence consists not in avoiding danger – which is impossible – but in correctly assessing particular threats and accepting the lesser evil as the better alternative.

Machiavelli has other advice for princes too: to choose ministers carefully, avoiding ones who are more ambitious for themselves than for the prince, and flatterers. Take advice, by all means, but once a policy has been decided upon, put it into action firmly and decisively. Otherwise, misled by flattery and the conflicting opinions of those following their own agenda, the leader will constantly change his mind and direction. As a result, he can do nothing properly and loses all esteem.

Although clearly a humanist and republican in his basic assumptions and values, Machiavelli also broke from that tradition in his concern for the practical realities of power, and the frank, unsentimental and (in Christian terms) amoral nature of his conclusions.

Actually, it is more accurate to say (as Isaiah Berlin has pointed out) that his work was shocking not because it was amoral or immoral, but because it was based on a completely different and competing morality: namely that of classical paganism, with its focus on the world rather than the soul, and on this world rather than the next.

I DIDN'T ARGUE THAT CHRISTIAN CONCERNS WERE UNIMPORTANT, OR THAT ITS UNDERSTANDING OF GOOD AND BAD WAS MISTAKEN

I SIMPLY MAINTAINED THAT IT IS IMPOSSIBLE TO BE BOTH A SUCCESSFUL CITIZEN AND A GOOD CHRISTIAN, SINCE AS THE FORMER YOU WILL HAVE TO DO THINGS THAT ARE REPREHENSIBLE TO THE LATTER.

THIS IS A DILEMMA THAT MANY PEOPLE WANTED TO IGNORE, AND STILL DO..

Machiavelli finishes **The Prince** with an "Exhortation to liberate Italy from the barbarians." Bewailing the condition of his native country –

...LEADERLESS, LAWLESS, CRUSHED, DESPOILED, TORN, OVERRUN...

Genoa

MILAN

Milan ● ● Pavia   Man

Parma ○

● Trent

VENICE

● Verona ● Vicenza
MIRANDOLA Padua

Modena

He says that the time is ripe for a new prince to arise, banishing the weakness and division that have made such humiliations possible. He quotes the Roman historian Livy: "Because a necessary war is a just war, and where there is hope only in arms, those arms are holy."

Machiavelli addresses this passionate appeal to Lorenzo de' Medici, urging him to raise a citizen army that will (unlike the mercenaries usually employed) be loyal and determined fighters in a great cause. All Italy, he

ALL ITALY WILL RALLY TO SUCH A SAVIOUR.

Siena

SIENA

cca · Florence

FLORENCE

Ferrara

Forlì · Urbino

Bologna · Città di Castello

Perugia

KINGDOM

OF NAPLES

ROME

· Rome

Naples

Prophet of the Risorgimento

The icy analyst Machiavelli reveals himself a romantic nationalist, a prophet of the **Risorgimento**, literally the "resurgence" in 19th century Italy, which finally brought independence and unification to the country.

> 350 YEARS LATER MY DREAM WAS MADE TRUE BY THE REPUBLICAN PATRIOTS GIUSEPPE MAZZINI (1805–72) AND GIUSEPPE GARIBALDI (1807–82).

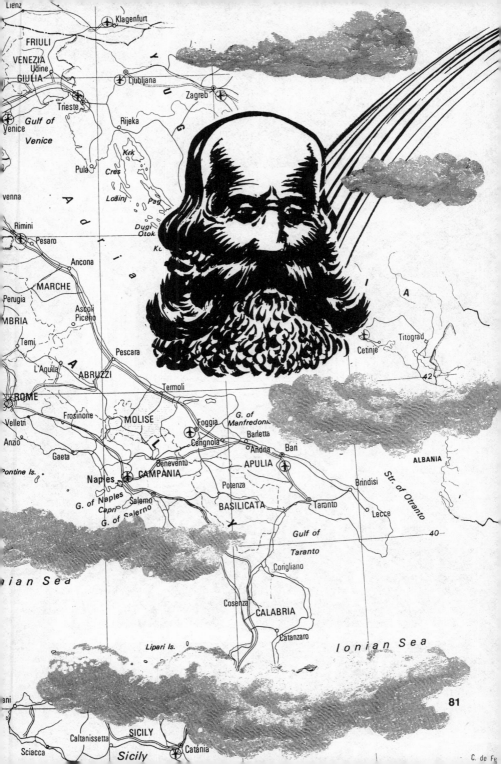

Sometime in 1514, Machiavelli realized that as a demonstration of his potential value to the government – let alone as a revolutionary call for national liberation – **The Prince** had fallen on deaf ears. Bitterly disappointed, he finally gave up hope of re-employment and turned increasingly to writing.

LORENZO DE' MEDICI THINKS ME TOO REPUBLICAN TO BE TRUSTED?

YOU MEAN, HE THINKS YOU TOO CLEVER BY HALF!

A Machiavellian Comedy

In 1518, Machiavelli wrote a witty black comedy, **La Mandragola** (**The Mandrake Root**). Successful performances followed in Rome and Florence over the next few years.

Callimaco, a handsome young man, returns from Paris to Florence to see for himself the much praised beauty, Lucrezia, young wife of the ageing lawyer Nicia Calfucci. Callimaco itches to possess Lucrezia, but she is as virtuous as Nicia is foolish.

Callimaco tells his servant Siro of a plan to infiltrate Nicia's house.

icia falls into the snare. The remedy Callir mandrake root.

Callimaco advises that they kidnap a healthy young man and put him in Lucrezia's bed for that one night. Nicia grudgingly agrees; but the trouble is to get Lucrezia to consent. Ligurio enlists the help of Lucrezia's father confessor, the corrupt Friar Timoteo, and her lewd mother Sostrata. Lucrezia at first rejects the idea.

The plan succeeds. Callimaco spends a night with Lucrezia and declares his undying love for her, and she proposes a continuing relationship. Everything ends happily for everyone, including the cuckolded Nicia who gains a child from all this chicanery.

Republican Friends: the Orti Oricellari

In about 1514, Machiavelli began to attend the literary and political discussions of a group of out-of-favour republicans. They met outside Florence at the gardens, the **Orti Oricellari**, of one of their members.

A SINGLE INDIVIDUAL, ACTING DECISIVELY AND RUTHLESSLY, MAY BE BEST SUITED TO ESTABLISHING OR RESTORING A STATE.

BUT A REPUBLIC COMPOSED OF MANY RULERS IS BEST FOR MAINTAINING AND PRESERVING IT.

These discussions in the Orti Oricellari stimulated Machiavelli to write a new book on which he spent five years, **The Discourses on the First Decade of Titus Livius**, based on the first ten books of the history of ancient Rome by Livy (59 BC–AD 17).

The Discourses . . .

The **Discourses** are Machiavelli's longest and perhaps most original political work. It is essential for a proper understanding of Machiavelli, because it clarifies two essential points.

FIRST, I NEVER URGED IMMORALITY FOR ITS OWN SAKE, BUT ONLY AS NECESSARY IN THE PURSUIT OF A STRONG, UNITED STATE...

SECOND, THE IDEAL FORM OF SUCH A STATE IS A REPUBLIC.

WE AGREE, OF COURSE, BUT ON WHAT DO YOU BASE YOUR REASONS?

... an Argument for Liberty

Although a constitutional monarchy may be a satisfactory compromise for a time, a republic is the best guarantee of maintaining the freedom and security of its citizens. Tyrannies, by contrast – whether as the rule of a single man or subjugation by a foreign power – result in weakness, poverty and decline.

EXPERIENCE SHOWS THAT CITIES HAVE NEVER INCREASED IN DOMINION EXCEPT WHILE THEY HAVE BEEN AT LIBERTY.

Liberty, in the form of self-government, is the ultimate goal that "excuses" any actions that help to bring it about. Note that Machiavelli's idea of liberty is not the modern one of an individual political "right".

In Machiavelli's opinion, the best example of this in human history was the Roman Republic. His goal, and his hope, is therefore to discover from its history "the practical lessons" needed to restore something of its success and glory today. Put very bluntly, **The Prince** offers advice to leaders for a secure state, whereas the **Discourses** offers advice to citizens for a free state.

As in **The Prince**, Machiavelli argues that it takes both good Fortune and **virtù** to achieve greatness. But here, the latter is something that must apply not just to the single ruler but to the whole citizenry.

The Case of Caesar

This explains why Machiavelli never misses an opportunity to criticize Julius Caesar, a dictator who replaced the Roman Republic with the Empire – despite his undoubted leadership qualities – and to excuse his assassins Brutus and Cassius. Because "when it is absolutely a question of the safety of one's country . . . there must be no consideration of just or unjust, of merciful or cruel, of praiseworthy or disgraceful.

Note that Machiavelli does not say that the end **justifies** the means, morally or otherwise; only that the end, when it is good, "excuses" the means.

For apart from just laziness and decadence, the chief danger to republican **virtù** is when either powerful individuals or small factions follow their own agenda at the expense of the collective public interest. Such corruption is ruinous to liberty, and it was the major concern of Machiavelli and republicans like him. This emphasis on collectivism – "a people is more prudent, more stable, and has better judgement than a prince" – was a departure from **The Prince**.

Trading the Future

Machiavelli's warning against the inherent danger of individual or factional self-interest is even more potent today. One example in 1995 was the spectacular fraud by Nick Leeson, a rogue trader heading the small Barings Futures operation in Singapore. He gambled away upwards of £600 million in "contracts" dealings on the Tokyo stock market and destroyed Barings, a London merchant bank in existence for 232 years. Such a costly example offers a glimpse into the heart of international banking and high finance.

Civic Duties

To protect against such private motivation, Machiavelli endorsed "good laws", including if necessary the severest penalties, to coerce citizens into preferring the common to the private good. The laws in this case are not about protecting individual rights, but are concerned with maintaining civic duties and punishing private bids for power. And along with this stick, there should be a carrot of consistently greater rewards for public than for private service.

Machiavelli was adamant that when men's reputations had been gained not by public service but "by private means, they are very dangerous and extremely harmful."

A Law unto Themselves

For this reason, Machiavelli was deeply suspicious of the nobility, despite the value of their martial prowess and spirit, because they stood above the law with estates and subjects of their own. He also thought that one of the likeliest sources of corruption was the ability of the rich to buy influence by means of patronage, nepotism and favours. The effect was to turn men from citizens into partisans, who look not to the public authority and public good but to that of a few others.

THUS FROM PARTISANS ARISE FACTIONS IN CITIES, FROM FACTIONS, THEIR RUIN.

A Modern Separatist Élite

A book by the American historian, Christopher Lasch, **The Revolt of the Élites** (1995), highlights an extreme new form of anti-civic "partnership" in line with Machiavelli's thought. Until recently, Lasch says, the economic and cultural élites of Western nation states were willing to shoulder civic responsibilities. Post-modern capitalism is characterized by a professional élite which defines itself as entirely separate from civic and national concerns. As Lasch argues, "the markets on which the fortunes of the new élites rely are tied to enterprises that operate across international boundaries . . . They have more in common with their counterparts in Brussels or Hong Kong than with the masses of people in their own country who are not yet plugged into the network of global communications."

WE PUT OUR MONEY INTO PRIVATE, SELF ENCLOSED ENCLAVES.

OUR KIDS GO TO PRIVATE SCHOOLS. WE HAVE OUR OWN PRIVATE SYSTEMS OF HEALTH, POLICE AND EVEN GARBAGE COLLECTION.

This privileged class (in America, the top 20 per cent) has made itself independent of the crumbling industrial cities and the public services in general.

Checks and Balances

So one of Machiavelli's key proposals for a "perfect republic" – taken from the institutional organisation of the Romans – was a mixed constitution, in which neither wealthy patricians nor the more numerous plebs could entirely dominate. Instead, each would "keep watch over the other", complementing each other's strengths, and (above all) preventing the triumph of factional interests.

MY IDEA OF CHECKS AND BALANCES LOOKS AHEAD TO THE AMERICAN CONSTITUTION.

This arrangement entails tolerating a certain amount of tension, disorder, and apparent disunity – things that other republican humanists, before and during Machiavelli's time, abhorred.

Even Machiavelli's friend, the diplomat Francesco Guicciardini (1483–1540), wrote:

Machiavelli's republicanism was not democratic in the modern sense; he was not particularly concerned to expand the enfranchisement of citizens beyond the minority that it was (perhaps five in one hundred). But he did believe in equality, in the sense of the vigorous participation of the "plebs", or ordinary citizens, in the political life of the ideal state.

Their brutalities are directed against those who have injured the common good, whereas those of princes are merely to defend their own good.   **103**

Religion is another resource for combating corruption and ensuring civic spirit – as much through fear as admiration. Characteristically, Machiavelli discusses how to make use of religious worship and its institutions for this purpose, as did the Romans.

COMPARE THE "CIVIC CULTS" OF THE ROMANS TO CHRISTIANITY AND ITS DISASTROUS EFFECTS IN ITALY – WEAKNESS, DIVISION AND THE TRIUMPH OF FOREIGN BARBARIANS!

The effects of a religion are what matter – not its "truth" or otherwise. This pragmatic approach, of course, scandalized the faithful.

Other-worldly Christianity

More specifically, where Christianity turned people away from this world, worship of the pagan gods had encouraged precisely **virtù**: strength, virility, skill, martial prowess and so on. It had also provided objects for sworn oaths that men feared to break; and divinatory omens which, when positive, filled armies with   the assurance of victory. By contrast,

...IF OUR RELIGION DEMANDS THAT YOU BE STRONG, WHAT IT ASKS FOR IS STRENGTH TO SUFFER, RATHER THAN STRENGTH TO DO BOLD THINGS.

Machiavelli does not argue that Christianity is wrong or untrue. As Isaiah Berlin puts it, "a man must choose . . . One can save one's soul, or one can found or maintain or serve a great and glorious state; but not always both at once."

Nor is Machiavelli necessarily cynical about religion. It is just that in his "religion" – classical paganism – both ethics and the sacred are inseparable from the social and political dimensions of human nature; as such, they contrast sharply with theist transcendence.

Of course, it shocked many that Machiavelli could propose pagan ideals more than a thousand years after the supposed triumph of Christian morality, and almost treat the latter as if it had never been, or was not particularly special, except perhaps for its ill effects on *human history!

An Argument for Imperialism

Machiavelli also held that the pursuit of dominance abroad fed into the maintenance of liberty at home, because "unless you are prepared to attack, you are liable to be attacked".

ARE YOU NOT CONCERNED ABOUT THE LOST LIBERTY OF THOSE DOMINATED ABROAD?

IF THEY CHERISH THEIR LIBERTY, IT WILL BE UP TO THEM TO FIGHT BACK.

Immigration

Interestingly enough, Machiavelli recommended easy access to citizenship by foreigners – that is, **immigration** – as a way to expand and renew the population.

Here again, Machiavelli insists on the importance of citizens' armies and has much to say about the wisest way to conduct wars. He ranges from arcane points of tactics, including the relative merits of infantry, cavalry and artillery, to advice of the most general and sensible kind, such as: keep your wars "short and big". But the basic lesson is that humility and forgiveness are usually unaffordable luxuries in the maintenance of liberty: "you can never hope to make yourself secure except by the exercise of power".

Machiavelli had serious doubts about the chances of long-term success, however. Humans tire even of stability and success, and crave novelty. They have a weakness, almost a flair, for corruption; and by the time it becomes visible, it has already taken hold in defiance of the old laws and measures. To restore **virtù** then requires extraordinary measures which very few are equal to carrying out.

> THE TROUBLE IS, MOST MEN PREFER TO STEER A MIDDLE COURSE, WHICH IS VERY HARMFUL; FOR THEY KNOW NOT HOW TO BE WHOLLY GOOD NOR WHOLLY BAD.

That is, they end up neither saving their souls nor adding to the stock of human glory here and now. Much better, he says, is "to be either magnificently bad or perfectly good."

In keeping with this mood, Machiavelli finishes the **Discourses** on a note almost of despair at the contrast between the Roman Republic and the stupidity of his own Italy, rulers and people alike. It is a sign of his profound ambivalence over whether the restoration of civic glory – supposedly the point of his book – was indeed possible.

IF THOSE CITY-STATES WHICH FROM THE OUTSET HAVE BEEN FREE, AS ROME WAS, FIND IT DIFFICULT TO FORMULATE LAWS WHEREBY TO MAINTAIN LIBERTY, THOSE WHICH HAVE JUST BEEN SERVILE ARE FACED WITH A NEAR — IMPOSSIBILITY.

Still, as Machiavelli poignantly justifies himself, "it is the duty of a good man to point out to others what is well done, even though the malignity of the times or of fortune has not permitted you to do it for yourself, so that of the many who have the capacity, some one, more beloved of heaven, may be able to do it."

Hope of Employment

In 1519, just as Machiavelli had finished his **Discourses**, Lorenzo de'Medici died. Shortly afterwards, his uncle Giulio became a cardinal and was soon to become Pope Clement VII.

Machiavelli kept writing. The next year, he was at work on a short treatise entitled **The Art of War**. This was interrupted in March, when he was finally introduced at the Medici court through the influence of Strozzi.

In November 1520, Machiavelli received a formal commission from Giulio de' Medici to write the history of Florence.

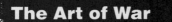

The Art of War

The Art of War appeared in 1521, dedicated to Strozzi. It was actually the only one of Machiavelli's books to be published in his lifetime. In it, Machiavelli repeats many of the themes we have already encountered. He argues that professional soldiers whose first allegiance is not to their country but to the army are a menace to everyone else in that country, since their loyalty is only to themselves, and their art is precisely violence and destruction.

THEY LACK THE KIND OF COMMITMENT — TO SAVE THEIR HOMES AND FAMILIES, END THE WAR AND GET BACK HOME — NEEDED TO BE REALLY EFFECTIVE SOLDIERS.

THEREFORE WAR SHOULD ONLY BE PRACTISED BY AN ARMED CITIZENRY, LED BY PUBLICLY APPOINTED LEADERS, AND UNDER PUBLIC AUTHORITY AND COMMAND?

Conversely, war teaches people the martial virtues of courage, discipline and action, which they need to be good citizens anyway. Here, once again, Machiavelli's sound advice looks forward to a model of the armed forces under constitutional control, without militaristic ambitions, which has contributed to the stability of the majority of Western democracies.

The Balancing Act

In 1522, a republican plot to assassinate the Medici Cardinal was discovered. The **Orti Oricellari** circle was scattered, with several members being exiled and one executed. This exposed (not for the last time) Machiavelli's delicate and dangerous balancing operation between his deeply felt republicanism and his need to keep in with the Medici, his sole hope of employment.

Medici

Republica

The History of Florence was finished in 1525, and Machiavelli travelled to Rome to present it to Clement VII.

Fortune and Misfortune

Meanwhile, Fortune was again abroad in the land. While Machiavelli was visiting Rome, Francis I of France was defeated and driven out of Italy by the imperial forces under Charles V of Spain. In the following year, 1526, Francis formed the Holy League with Pope Clement.

FRANCE

Francis I

CHARLES V

THAT SAME YEAR, 1526, I WAS FINALLY APPOINTED AN OFFICIAL OF THE FLORENTINE GOVERNMENT AND ASKED TO UNDERTAKE SOME DIPLOMATIC WORK.

SIENA

ROMA

PISA

In May of 1527, Charles V responded to the new French challenge by sending his armies – a mixture of Spanish troops with Italian and German mercenaries – back into Italy.

BUT THEY WERE BADLY PAID AND UNDISCIPLINED, AND, INSTEAD OF ATTACKING MILITARY TARGETS, THEY SACKED ROME ITSELF.

Clement VII was obliged to flee, and, without his backing, the Medici regime in Florence crumbled.

In a typically bitter twist of Fortune, however, the new generation of republicans passed over Machiavelli as someone who had been tainted by too close an association with the Medici.

HOW CAN THEY DOUBT MY REPUBLICAN SINCERITY? THIS IS TOO MUCH!

This last blow may have undermined Machiavelli's health, for on 2[...] [...] 1527, after a short illness, he died. Rumours quickly spread of a deathbed confession to a priest, but there is no evidence supporting this, which seems to have been Catholic disinformation. He was buried the next day in Santa Croce, at the heart of his beloved Florence.

The extraordinary turbulence which marked Machiavelli's life continued immediately afterwards.

In 1531, four years after Machiavelli's death, the **Discourses** was published; and, the following year, both **The Prince** and **The History of Florence**. Exactly two decades later, the first Index of books prohibited by the Catholic Church appeared.

AT THE INSTIGATION OF THE JESUITS, IT INCLUDED ALL OF MY BOOKS!

☆G!✕ DAMN THO WITH THEIR AND EV @F @!! CENSORED CENSORED

But the next year, they started to appear in Latin, published in Protestant Basle, Switzerland.

The first English translation of the **Discourses** did not appear until 1636, and of **The Prince**, not until four years later. But these were the first of many that have been published right up to the present.

Machiavelli Applied in Practice

As we have seen, Machiavelli's reputation as a diabolical apostle of intrigue, duplicity and power politics is a travesty of his actual work. Nonetheless, it is very tempting to take this route, sticking purely to **The Prince** without any bigger context and "applying" it to modern politics.

The Way of the Fox

There are many possible examples in recent history. One is the way General Francisco Franco (1892–1975) used the possibility of Spain's entry into World War II to play the Rome–Berlin Axis off against the Allied Powers by giving strictly limited support to Hitler while at the same time accepting aid from the Allies.

THAT'S HOW HE STAYED IN POWER FOR OVER 35 YEARS!

The Iron Lady

One of the most successful contemporary politicians, the former British Prime Minister Margaret Thatcher, has been described as an instinctive Machiavellian. (There is, however, no evidence that she ever actually read him.)

Certainly, the Falklands War was a masterpiece of manipulation, a short and spectacular victory which she then used to steamroller opponents of her domestic legislative programmes.

It was her own ex-Chancellor of the Exchequer and ex-Foreign Secretary, not the Opposition, who eventually brought her down.

Lord McAlpine, Mrs Thatcher's former deputy chairman and loyal acolyte, has already produced an advice book for would-be politicians and their supporters entitled **The Servant: A New Machiavelli**.

I'M AT WORK ON A BOOK APPLYING MACHIAVELLISM TO AMERICAN CORPORATE TAKEOVERS AND MERGERS.

YOU IGNORE THE AWKWARD FACT THAT I ALWAYS ABHORRED PRIVATE PROFIT AND FORECAST DOOM FOR ANY SOCIETY WHICH PERMITS IT TO FLOURISH!

Indeed, his dictum of keeping "the public rich and citizens poor" seems clearly enough to imply some form of what we would call socialism!

Charles de Gaulle was a master of playing both sly fox and roaring lion. François Mitterrand, following in his footsteps, is another example of a contemporary Prince. But Mikhail Gorbachev erred badly in first humiliating Boris Yeltsin, then overlooking his rise to power. And Bill Clinton is in serious danger of personifying Machiavelli's warning about the irresolute Prince who "is constantly changing his mind because of conflicting advice". He thus risks becoming an object of scorn and contempt.

This way of using Machiavelli is fun and instructive, but it is also relatively superficial. It ignores his fundamental commitments to active citizenship and political participation. So it is also in danger of missing the most important lessons he has to offer.

Machiavelli's Lessons

Machiavelli grappled with more than just politics, of course. War, for example

A bad example is the civil war in former Yugoslavia and the involvement of the United Nations in it.

NEVER DELAY WAR WHEN IT IS INEVITABLE. TO DO SO MERELY PLAYS INTO YOUR OPPONENTS' HANDS.

Donald Kagan, an eminent American historian of war, recently drew the very Machiavellian conclusion that "Peace does not keep itself". Rather, it depends not only on the maintenance of a credible deterrent, but the readiness to "act realistically while there is time", rather than waiting "until there is no choice but war".

131

Machiavelli and the Foundation of the Modern Political Theory of Civic Republicanism

It is in political and social theory that Machiavelli's presence continues to be most felt.

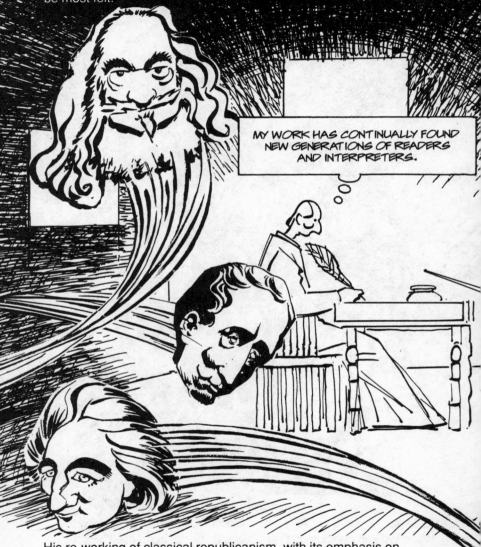

His re-working of classical republicanism, with its emphasis on participatory citizenship and its hostility to the corruption of factional and private gain, gave this tradition a new lease of life in the modern world of the nation-state.

But civic republicanism has had powerful competition from other traditions, often hostile. And it suffers from other misunderstandings too.

DON'T CONFUSE IT WITH THE REPUBLICAN PARTY IN THE *USA* — OR THE *IRA* (IRISH REPUBLICAN ARMY)!

Machiavellian America

One strand of Machiavelli's thought reached early America through the writings of the political philosopher of the French Enlightenment, Charles Montesquieu (1689–1755). By this route, Machiavelli's civic republicanism influenced the founding fathers of American Independence.

WE BELIEVED THAT WITH A CONFEDERAL REPUBLIC ...

Thomas Jefferson (1743–1826)

James Madison (1751–1836)

...LINKING TOGETHER STATES WITH CONSIDERABLE INDEPENDENT POWERS (I.E. MINI-REPUBLICS) ...

These founding fathers of the United States of America were at once products and classic figures of the Enlightenment which had such immense social and political impact on the West.

George Washington (1732–99)

The Social Contract

In Europe, Jean-Jacques Rousseau (1712–78) tried to replace the civic virtue of fellow citizens with virtuous laws, established by common consent. The effect of this was to turn Machiavelli's emphasis on the public and social (over private and individual) into the potentially authoritarian concept of "the general will" – something which passed via the French Revolution into the ideas of Marx.

MAN MUST BE FORCED TO BE FREE.

IS THAT WHAT YOU MEAN BY THE "SOCIAL CONTRACT"?

Frederick the Great (1712–86), King of Prussia, as "enlightened despot", wrote **Antimachiavell** in 1740 to defend humanity against "this monster who wants to destroy it". Twelve years later, after some experience of governing, he wrote differently.

IN IMPORTANT RESPECTS, I AM FORCED TO ADMIT THAT MACHIAVELLI IS RIGHT.

As for Napoleon Bonaparte (1769–1821) . . .

THE PRINCE IS THE ONLY BOOK WORTH READING.

G.W.F. Hegel (1770–1831) commended Machiavelli for anticipating the importance or the modern nation state, which Hegel saw as the direct heir of the classical republic.

Karl Marx (1818–83) inherited Enlightenment influences and the historicism of Hegel which he "inverted" by replacing the idealism of the Universal Spirit with the materialism of forces and relations of production.

But that did not fundamentally alter the potential tyranny in such a theory and practice, when the state actually replaces and acts for the people, the party for the state, and eventually the leader for the party.

Post-Modern Machiavelli

The irony here is that Machiavelli's chief obsession, and the point for him of a republic, was the liberty of its actual, not ideal, citizens. Nor can Machiavelli's value-pluralism (as Isaiah Berlin has pointed out) be reconciled with such monism and rationalism, whether in Hegel's idealist system or Marx's materialist version.

THAT IS WHY, UNLIKE YOU, I FELT UNDER NO OBLIGATION TO PRETEND THAT ONLY ONE SET OF VALUES WAS TRUE, AND THAT ANY OTHERS — CHRISTIAN, FOR INSTANCE — WERE "REALLY" MISTAKEN; OR THAT I KNEW BETTER THAN PEOPLE THEMSELVES WHAT IS GOOD FOR THEM. THE POINT IS PRECISELY FOR CITIZENS TO DECIDE THINGS FOR THEMSELVES.

In view of the history of the 20th century, this is a colossal virtue. Equally, in the light of post-modern pluralism, pragmatism and relativism, it leaves Machiavelli looking much the most progressive thinker.

Let's briefly examine the root problems of civic republicanism which post-modern theory has inherited and must reconsider.

Civic Virtue versus Civil Society

Civic virtue has also suffered, both in history and in theory, from the rise of what is (confusingly) called "civil society" – that is, that part of society consisting of voluntary associations for mutual benefit, whether commercial or otherwise.

THE OPPOSITE OF CIVIL SOCIETY IS USUALLY CONSIDERED TO BE RELATIONS INSTITUTED OR REQUIRED BY THE STATE.

AND WHAT ARE THE SUPPOSED BENEFITS OF THIS "CIVIL SOCIETY"?

CHARLES MONTESQUIEU 1639~1755

Let's take the example of Montesquieu, who thought Machiavelli's republicanism asked too much of people.

YOUR CIVIC VIRTUE CAN LARGELY BE REPLACED BY A THRIVING CIVIL SOCIETY IN WHICH THE REWARDS FOR GOOD SOCIAL BEHAVIOUR ARE SO GREAT THAT NO GREAT CIVIC VIRTUE IS REQUIRED.

Alexis de Tocqueville (1805–59) came along later and agreed with Montesquieu.

A GOOD EXAMPLE OF THIS PROCESS IS MID – 19TH CENTURY AMERICA WHERE A FREE MARKET ECONOMY IS WELL UNDERWAY AND RADICALLY ALTERING ITS ORIGINAL REPUBLICAN ASSUMPTIONS.

143

The Free Market

The rise of civil society – increasingly dominated by commerce and business – received another huge boost from the influential 18th-century "Scottish Enlightenment", especially Adam Smith (1723–90). He too praised voluntary associations (hence "free") for purposes of mutual private gain (hence "market").

THE FREE MARKET WILL TURN INCORRIGIBLE HUMAN SELFISHNESS INTO THE "CIVIL" AND TOLERANT BEHAVIOUR OF "ENLIGHTENED SELF INTEREST".

BUT THIS CAN ONLY LEAD TO THE FACTIONAL NEGLECT OF CIVIC RESPONSIBILITIES.

Republican Critics of the Free Market

Republicans, however – like Thomas Paine (1737–1809) and William Cobbett (1763–1835) – viewed the same developments as mostly a potent new manifestation of the aristocratic "Old Corruption".

Post-Communist Civil Society

The dissidents of Communist Eastern Europe and the USSR held out great hopes for civil society, where it had been crushed by Marxist-Leninist regimes as a threat to the authority of the state.

ISN'T IT TRUE THAT THE POST COMMUNIST SOCIETIES ARE MUCH FREER NOW?

BUT THESE HOPES HAVE MOSTLY COME TO GRIEF, AS A RESULT OF THE SAME PROBLEM: THE EXTENT TO WHICH CIVIL SOCIETY IS AT THE MERCY OF PROFIT— DRIVEN PRIVATE BUSINESS AND CONSUMERIST INDIVIDUALISM.

"No Such Thing as Society"

The results of the free market in both East and West are not only not particularly "civil", but, as Mrs Thatcher has famously said, not even a "society".

147

The Origins of Liberal Democracy

Civic republicanism has also been eclipsed by what is the dominant modern political discourse, that of modern liberal democracy. It is associated with the idea of individual "natural rights" and a social contract between people and rulers. Its origins lie largely in the work of two philosophers.

One was Thomas Hobbes (1588–1679).

I WAS A MONARCHIST ABSOLUTIST AND PIONEERED THE IDEA OF A BINDING CONTRACT BETWEEN RULER AND SUBJECTS — NOT CITIZENS.

In both the content and abstract style of his **Leviathan** (1651), Hobbes showed contempt for history, civic participation, and mixed or constitutional government.

I WROTE *OCEANA* IN *1656*, A REPUBLICAN UTOPIA INTENDED TO COUNTER *HOBBES*, BUT IT WAS LESS INFLUENTIAL.

The other was the political philosopher John Locke (1632–1704). In his **Two Treatises of Government** (1690), Locke insisted on the right to property and to rebellion against a ruler if necessary. But he added further weight to the idea both of individuals and their rights and of a contract under which the people surrender much of their power to a ruler and his ministers or magistrates.

IN THIS TRADITION, INDIVIDUALS ARE MUCH MORE IMPORTANT THAN COMMUNITIES.

AND THEY ARE THE BEARERS OF "RIGHTS", REGARDLESS OF WHAT THEY DO, WHICH ARE GUARANTEED BY THE STATE, WHICH IN TURN IS RUN BY DEMOCRATICALLY ELECTED REPRESENTATIVES.

TWO TREATISES OF GOVERNMENT
JOHN LOCKE

SOUNDS TO ME LIKE TOO MANY ABSTRACT FRAGMENTS — "INDIVIDUALS", "RIGHTS" "STATE", "REPRESENTATIVES"...

149

Modern Liberal Democracy

In practice, liberal democracy has usually gone together with so-called free-market economics. During the Cold War era, from about 1945 to 1989, both were opposed by the Soviet Bloc Marxism and its planned "command" economies. These socialist economies were already fast crumbling away in the 1980s. This was also the decade of Conservative free-market **monetarism**, theorized by Milton Friedman and put into political practice by Ronald Reagan and Mrs Thatcher.

In 1992, the American historian Francis Fukuyama proclaimed the Hegelian new gospel of liberal democracy in his book **The End of History and the Last Man**. Fukuyama's doctrine asserts that the "end of history", that is, its goals, is none other than liberal democracy and the free market – globally!

LIBERAL DEMOCRACY IS THE ONLY COHERENT POLITICAL ASPIRATION THAT SPANS DIFFERENT REGIONS AND CULTURES AROUND THE GLOBE... IT CANNOT BE IMPROVED UPON.

I HAVE NEVER SEEN ANYTHING POLITICAL THAT CAN'T BE IMPROVED UPON!

What Becomes of "Civic Virtue"?

But the essence of civic virtue is citizens' ruling themselves. So, from that point of view, neither style of government is very satisfactory. It is true that democracy involves more people; and, to that extent, republicanism favours it over any kind of oligarchy (rule by a few) . . .

But when democracy means little more than voting every four or five years for parties whose main difference is wanting to run the economy slightly more or less humanely, then a republican would say that something is very wrong.

...IN MY DAY, USUALLY THE ARISTOCRACY, BUT A POLITICALLY CORRECT ÉLITE IS NO DIFFERENT IN ESSENCE.

AND A SOCIETY OF POSSESSIVE, ALIENATED, ISOLATED INDIVIDUALS, AT THE MERCY OF GLOBAL CAPITAL, CONFIRMS THE DIAGNOSIS.

Republicanism of the Left and Right?

Republicanism has never sat comfortably with the superficial but almost universal political opposition of "left" and "right", terms which originated in the French Revolution. The former socialist republics of Eastern Europe, including those in the Soviet Union, were not properly speaking "republican". Nor indeed are right-wing ones, such as the fundamentalist Islamic state of Iran.

A Right-wing Machiavellian

Benito Mussolini (1883–1945), founder of Fascism and Italian dictator, began his political career on the left as a leader of the revolutionary wing of the Italian Socialist Party (PSI). In World War I, he broke with the PSI's policy of neutrality, supported the war and abandoned his socialist beliefs. He rose to power by a crafty strategy of party politics, King Victor Emmanuel III's tacit support and the use of Fascist terror squads, culminating in the March on Rome in 1922 and total dictatorship in 1926.

A Left-wing Machiavellian

Antonio Gramsci (1891–1937), a founder of the Italian Communist Party in 1921 and, in 1924, a member of the Italian parliament, witnessed the left's crushing defeats – its failures in post-war Europe to imitate Lenin's seizure of power in Russia; the downfall of social-democratic socialism in the 1930s; and the fiasco of his own involvement in the mass industrial Turin factory councils of 1918–20. Gramsci was imprisoned by Mussolini's Fascist regime from 1926 to his death in 1927. He mainly wrote his theories in prison, including a 300-page volume of **Notes on Machiavelli**.

Gramsci's Rethinking of Marxism

Marx himself had concentrated on the economic analysis of capitalism and left no blueprint of how a socialist government would actually function. Marxists were only concerned with the revolutionary moment of a transfer of power to socialism – what happened after that moment had no connection with what had gone on before.

But Gramsci, through his re-reading of Machiavelli, foresaw the crisis that a seizure of power would bring.

Gramsci, despite his prison "defeat" by Fascism, proved more far-sightedly Machiavellian. On 28 April 1945, Mussolini was shot [...] partisans of the Italian Resistance. Before his execution, he said . [...]

Post-Modern Gramsci
"The People is the Prince"

Gramsci's idea – "the People is the Prince" – is a contribution to a possible Machiavellian socialist republic.

He considered what was **absent** in Marx's own theory and in Lenin's attempt to create a communist state in Russia, and these absences can now be seen as prophecies of the very defects that would lead to the collapse of the Soviet Union, the discrediting of Marxism and the defeat even of reformist parliamentary socialism.

Socialist states created by Lenin, Stalin, Mao and others relied on the mechanisms of a state-managed economy which excluded the mass of the people from the civic responsibilities of **politics**. They failed to create either socialist or civil societies.

If you exclude the people from participation, marginalize them, threaten their identity and nationhood, you will inevitably get sabotage and a conservative response.

Obvious post-modern elements in Gramsci's thinking are: decentralization, pluralist participation and respect for popular culture. He grew suspicious of modernist Utopianism which lacks organic contact with the social reality it wishes to transform. Socialism constructed without a civic-republican base will be the sort of modern architecture that no one wants to live in.

Communitarianism

Increasingly, with the collapse of socialism as a plausible alternative, the much needed critique of liberal democracy has come instead from "communitarians": philosophers such as Alisdair MacIntyre, Michael Walzer, Robert Bellah and most recently Amitai Etzioni.

"COMMUNITARIANS" MAINTAIN THAT IF SOCIETY AND EVEN DEMOCRACY ARE TO WORK, THEY NEED STRONG COMMUNITY TIES AND PLENTY OF CIVIC VIRTUE.

RIGHTS SHOULD THEREFORE BE ACCOMPANIED BY SOCIAL RESPONSIBILITIES, AND WE NEED A CONCEPT OF "THE COMMON GOOD".

WE EMPHASIZE OUR INTERDEPENDENCE, OUR EMBEDDEDNESS IN VARIOUS COMMUNITIES, THE DUTIES WE OWE TO EACH OTHER AS WELL AS THE ADVANTAGES OF MUTUAL SOLIDARITY...

...AND THE IMPORTANCE OF ECONOMIC, POLITICAL AND CULTURAL LOCALISM.

A typical conclusion is that of Robert D. Putnam: "strong and free government depends on a virtuous and public-spirited citizenry". It is highly appropriate that his book, **Making Democracy Work**, is subtitled **Civic Traditions in Modern Italy**.

SO FAR, I WOULD WHOLEHEARTEDLY AGREE.

But there are two problems with communitarianism.

FIRST, IT IS STRONG ON COMMUNITY BUT WEAKER ON CITIZENSHIP.

TRUE, LIBERAL DEMOCRACY IS IN DANGER OF PRODUCING A NON-SOCIETY OF PASSIVE AND ISOLATED INDIVIDUALS.

BUT COMMUNITARIANS RISK PRODUCING AN ALTERNATIVE OF REGRESSIVE COMMUNITIES, BASED ON ETHNIC AND OTHER EXCLUSIVE IDENTITIES, WHICH ARE INTERNALLY REPRESSIVE AND EXTERNALLY HOSTILE.

APPEALING TO ARISTOTELIAN AND RIGIDLY SOCIAL CONCEPTS OF "HUMAN NATURE" IMPLIES A READINESS TO SACRIFICE THE INDIVIDUAL FOR THE COMMUNITY.

COMMUNITARIANS NEED TO THINK MORE ABOUT HOW TO OVERCOME THIS DANGER THROUGH ENCOURAGING THE PRACTICES OF CITIZENSHIP. THESE PRACTICES SHOULD BE SOCIALLY INCLUSIVE, RATHER THAN EXCLUSIVE, AND FORWARD-LOOKING, RATHER THAN "SHORT-TERMIST".

NOR IS A TYRANNICAL COLLECTIVITY WHAT I ADVOCATED.

As Quentin Skinner has pointed out, in Machiavelli's republicanism one of the main reasons for maintaining public virtù is so that individually we are free to do what wish.

The second problem is that, like advocates of "civil society", communitarians often fail to recognize the extent to which commercial market forces are now able to corrupt communities.

Sometimes the debate between liberals and their critics has taken the form of a debate between advocates of "negative liberty" – the right to freedom **from** undue constraint on doing what one wants – and proponents of "positive freedom" – the right to **have** or **do** various specific things and, as far as possible, actually to be provided with the necessary means. (Isaiah Berlin and Richard Rorty represent the former view; Charles Taylor, among others, represents the latter.)

WITHOUT THE ABILITY TO ACTUALLY DO THINGS, FREEDOM IS EMPTY AND EVEN CYNICAL.

BUT SUCH "SOCIAL RIGHTS" LEAD TO THE STULTIFYING IMPOSITION OF A BUREAUCRATIC AND ULTIMATELY AUTHORITARIAN UNIFORMITY.

SO WE HAVE STALEMATE.

BURGER KING

Here too, Machiavelli offers a solution.

OUR COMMON CIVIC DUTIES ARE SIMPLY NECESSARY TO PRESERVE OUR INDIVIDUAL FREEDOM. SO BOTH ARE EQUALLY IMPORTANT, WHEN CORRECTLY UNDERSTOOD.

Republicanism Now

It is clear that civic republicanism is highly critical of modern liberal democracy, with its over-emphasis on the individual. But, equally clearly, it does not argue for a return to collectivism, socialist or otherwise.

THE KEY CONCEPT IS *CITIZENSHIP.*

AND THAT MEANS AN END TO THE DESTRUCTIVE ILLUSION OF THE "PRIVATE CITIZEN".

It has sometimes been argued that the (post-)modern world is too different (that is, too complex, or too big) from the ancient city-state for republicanism to work. And it is true that there is no longer any **one** community. We are all members of many communities, actual and potential, all the way from communities at an international, even cross-species, level to those at the most local, neighbourhood level.

BUT THIS IS NOT NECESSARILY A PROBLEM.

IT MEANS THAT INSTEAD OF THE OLD FUNDAMENTALIST MONISMS THAT HAVE PROVED SO DESTRUCTIVE (RELIGIOUS, SOCIAL, POLITICAL), PLURALISM IS A NECESSARY PART OF CONTEMPORARY CITIZENSHIP.

And plural communities actually invite such a practice. For, as Adrian Oldfield puts it, "what size and complexity do . . . is to multiply the opportunities for citizen involvement and action."

Another related objection is that there is now too little sense of community to sustain republicanism. But this is to ignore the opposite.

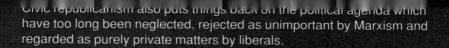

Civic republicanism also puts things back on the political agenda which have too long been neglected, rejected as unimportant by Marxism and regarded as purely private matters by liberals.

THINGS LIKE MORAL AND CIVIC EDUCATION, AND EVEN RELIGION.

I WAS VERY CLEAR THAT RELIGION COULD PLAY A CRUCIAL ROLE, FOR GOOD OR ILL, IN MAINTAINING CIVIC VIRTUE.

Other major challenges include the redefinition of work as a contribution to the good of all, as opposed to merely being a matter of pure self- advancement.

Machiavelli Now

None of this would surprise Machiavelli, if he were miraculously transported into the present. What else might he say? Obviously we can only speculate, but, in the first place, while remarking on the obvious and spectacular changes from his day – especially scientific and technological – he would probably add, with some grim satisfaction, that basic human nature seemed to have changed very little.

COLLECTIVELY SPEAKING, PEOPLE STILL TEND TO BEHAVE IN WAYS WHOSE EFFECTS ARE STUPID, SHORT-SIGHTED, AND A MENACE NOT ONLY TO EACH OTHER AND OTHER LIFE-FORMS BUT TO THE HEALTH OF THE PLANET AS A WHOLE.

Then he might ask, what did we expect when, even in so called democratic countries, we have become so selfish and passive, letting factions of tiny, powerful and unaccountable élites dominate both politics and economics? That applies to most leading political parties, even in democracies, whose overriding concerns usually seem to be getting re-elected and protecting big business.

SUCH A TRIUMPH OF PARTICULAR INTERESTS, ABLE TO REWARD THEIR OWN BEYOND THE DREAMS OF THOSE PURSUING THE COMMON GOOD, IS, OF COURSE, THE PERFECT RECIPE FOR CORRUPTION. AND WITH THE LOSS OF CIVIC *VIRTÙ* GOES OUR LIBERTY — WHICH, OF COURSE, PERFECTLY SUITS OUR RULERS.

Machiavelli would also instantly recognize our "culture industry" for what it mostly is.

Finally, he would be amazed at our complacency about our precious "rights". Machiavelli's warning is clear.

"If modern Machiavellism should be questioned, as indeed it should, the questioning must begin with modernity itself. For one thing should be clear by now: by attacking Machiavelli one cannot save the world from the Machiavellism of modernity."

Anthony Parel, **The Machiavellian Cosmos** (New Haven, Yale University Press, 1992).

Further Reading

The standard English edition is Allan Gilbert (editor), *Machiavelli: the Chief Works and Others* (Durham NC, Duke University Press, 1965). The standard biography is R. Ridolfi, *The Life of Niccolò Machiavelli*, translated by Colin Grayson (London, Routledge & Kegan Paul, 1963). See also Sebastian de Grazia, *Machiavelli in Hell* (Hemel Hempstead, Harvester Wheatsheaf, 1989, and London, Picador, 1992).

The best short work on Machiavelli's life and work is Quentin Skinner, *Machiavelli* (Oxford, Oxford University Press, 1981).

There are several translations of *The Prince* available, including those of George Bull (London, Penguin, 1981) and Quentin Skinner and Russell Price (Cambridge, Cambridge University Press, 1988); and one of *The Discourses*, Bernard Crick (editor) (London, Penguin, 1970).

Other excellent works are: J. G. A. Pocock, *The Machiavellian Moment: Florentine Political Thought and the Atlantic Republican Tradition* (Princeton, Princeton University Press, 1975), and Gisela Bock, Quentin Skinner and Maurizio Viroli (editors), *Machiavelli and Republicanism* (Cambridge, Cambridge University Press, 1990).

Books applying Machiavelli to modern politics include Alistair McAlpine, *The Servant: A New Machiavelli* (London, Faber & Faber, 1992), and Edward Pearce, *Machiavelli's Children* (London, Victor Gollancz, 1993).

The quotations by Isaiah Berlin are from "The Originality of Machiavelli", pp. 25–79 in his *Against the Current* H. Hardy (editor) (Oxford, Clarendon Press, 1981). Other passages quoted or mentioned: Donald Kagan, *On the Origins of War and the Preservation of Peace* (New York, Doubleday, 1995); Robert D. Putnam, *Making Democracy Work: Civic Traditions in Modern Italy* (Princeton, Princeton University Press, 1995); and Adrian Oldfield's excellent *Citizenship and Community: Civic Republicanism and the Modern World* (London, Routledge, 1990).

Oscar Zarate thanks Hazel Hirshorn and Maria Reidy at the Italian Culture Institute for picture research.

Additional drawings on pages 83–85 by Woodrow Phoenix.

Patrick Curry is a freelance writer and historian living in London. His interests include the history of astrology, literary criticism, politics and ecology.

Oscar Zarate, winner of the 1994 Will Eisner Prize for comicstrip illustration, has many internationally acclaimed titles to his credit, including *Fatlips*, a children's book with Arnold Wesker, the graphic novels of Shakespeare's *Othello*, Marlowe's *Dr Faustus, Geoffrey the Tube Train and the Fat Comedian* with Alexei Sayle and *A Small Killing* with Alan Moore. His previous titles with Icon Books are the best-selling *Freud for Beginners*, as well as the classic *Lenin* and more recent *Mafia* and *Stephen Hawking for Beginners*.

Lettering by Woodrow Phoenix.
Typesetting by Wayzgoose.